The Feather
and the Furrow

The Feather and the Furrow

The bird photographs of CHRIS KNIGHTS

Edited by ROBIN PAGE

BIRD'S FARM BOOKS

Published by Bird's Farm Books, Barton, Cambridgeshire CB3 7AG
www.crtbarton.org.uk
Distributed by Merlin Unwin Books, 7 Corve Street, Ludlow, Shropshire SY8 1DB
Order Line 01584 877456

ISBN 0 905232 20 8

Designed by Jim Reader and Tim McPhee
Design and production in association with Book Production Consultants plc,
25–27 High Street, Chesterton, Cambridge CB4 1ND
www.bpccam.co.uk

Printed and bound in Great Britain by The Burlington Press, Foxton, Cambridge

FRONTISPIECE: A barn owl hunting.

Contents

Dedication

I would like to dedicate this book to my wife Jo for all her patience, understanding and good humour. To be married to a farmer requires all three virtues; but being married to a farmer/photographer requires even larger quantities than usual.

Acknowledgements

Most of the figures I have quoted in this book have come from that excellent volume *The State of the Nations' Birds* by Chris Meads, and cover the last 25 years. I have also quoted from *A History of British Birds* by that wonderful old naturalist and wood engraver Thomas Bewick (1753–1828). I would like to thank English Nature, who, over the years, have helped me to obtain the necessary permits to take many of the photographs in this book.

There are several people whose efforts have been indispensable in producing *The Feather and the Furrow*. I would like to thank Sarah and Margaret for typing the text, Jim Reader and Tim McPhee for their excellent design and to Franca Holden for overseeing the whole thing on behalf of Book Production Consultants.

Foreword

For years farmers have had a bad reputation. As farming has become more intensive, populations of farmland wildlife have plummeted as a direct result because of disturbance, habitat destruction and chemical use – farmers have been blamed for the changes that have occurred. They have been accused of being greedy, short sighted and environmentally illiterate. No doubt some farmers are guilty of all three sins – but the direction farming has taken over recent decades has not been driven by farmers – it has simply followed political direction. Consequently, when environmentalists mourn the loss of the skylark, or the English (grey) partridge, they should not be blaming the average farmer – they should be blaming the politicians who put the flawed policies into place, and the agri-businessmen who supported them. They are reluctant of course to place the blame where it belongs because so many of them are dependent on the Government for grants and influence – and many of them regard the 'ear of the minister' as being far more important than 'rocking the boat', so money dominates environmental politics just as it does agriculture.

Fortunately not all farmers go with the flow. One of these is Chris Knights, who farms in the Brecks of Norfolk. At first glance Chris Knights is a 'big farmer', farming 9000 acres of Norfolk; at some seasons he employs 800 people, and his farming methods can be as intensive as anywhere in Britain – or indeed the world. But at second glance things are slightly different; Chris Knights was not born with a silver spoon in his mouth, and in fact his father was born in a converted hen house. He has a broad Norfolk accent and is proud of his Norfolk heritage, and high up over his Norfolk farm larks sing during the summer.

Yes, Chris Knights farms intensively – but he did not follow – he led the way in producing carrots, parsnips and lettuces by the million using the latest technology and science – and developing some of his own. But as he built up his farm, he has also become one of the top wildlife film-

OPPOSITE: *A 'conservation headland', full of wildflowers (weeds) on the farm of Chris Knights.*

ABOVE: *Irrigation – the intensive side of farming.*
OPPOSITE: *The grey partridge – the conservation side of farming.*

makers, bird photographers and conservationists in the country. At the same time as he has been producing high volume vegetables for supermarkets and shopping chains he has been farming for some of Britain's most endangered wildlife. Consequently, among the fields of high-tech farming there are stone curlews, lapwings, ringed plovers, English (grey) partridges, barn owls, brown hares and skylarks – all species on a very slippery slope over most of Britain – but flourishing on the farm of Chris Knights and his sons.

His high-tech fields give high yields, but if the stone curlews get to a 50-acre field before the carrot drill, the stone curlews get the field. Similarly, if a lapwing or a stone curlew nests before the plough arrives, then feathers take precedence over the furrow and the plough has to go round the eggs – or the eggs are moved carefully to one side onto the newly ploughed land so that the nesting bird can resume incubation as soon as the plough has passed by.

The interest of Chris Knights in nature is not new, and he made space for wildlife on his farm long before 'agri-environment schemes' (subsidies for wildlife) had been thought of by the bureaucrats.

OPPOSITE: *The skylark – a sign of sustainable farming.*
ABOVE: *The lapwing – under pressure, but not on this Norfolk farm.*

His love of wildlife started as a small boy, and he remembers entering a 'Bird and Tree' competition run by the RSPB and the Wildfowl Trust while at primary school. It was an essay about lapwings and ash trees – he claims that it is the only thing he has written until *The Feather and the Furrow* – and he received a medal for his efforts.

He started taking photographs when he was 14. With the arrival of a Frances Barnet motorbike, at the age of 16, the north Norfolk coast came within range of his camera and he has not looked back since. In the course of his photography he got to know a number of famous artists and conservationists including R.A. Richardson, the Norfolk artist John Harrison and Peter Scott.

In 1965 he bought his first movie camera and life became even more hectic, as film-making had to be fitted in around farming. While filming he met a builder from Doncaster who also dabbled with wildlife films. It was the start of a life-long friendship and collaboration with Terry Andrewartha, another film-maker and naturalist of immense talent and knowledge. They were the

last 'do-it-yourself' part-time film-makers and made a number of famous films together for Anglia Television's *Survival* series, including programmes on the roe deer, brown hare, capercaillie in Scotland and grey partridge.

It was lack of time that turned Chris away from films and back to still photography. Running a farm is time consuming and Chris could not squeeze enough into 24 hours. Nevertheless, he won the Bird Photographer of the Year competition in 1985 for his stunning picture of a great crested grebe (see page 94), and his pictures appear in magazines, journals and books all over the world. His dual careers as farmer and film-maker have been of mutual benefit. His farming and wildlife knowledge helped his film-making. Then, greater study of wildlife from the camera has helped his farming. He began to see what wildlife needed to survive and flourish, and so he incorporated what he learnt while filming into his farming practices.

The presence of healthy populations of grey partridges, lapwings, and skylarks show the success of Chris Knights' philosophy of farming. All three birds are regarded as 'indicator species', and over the last twenty-five years the grey partridge population has fallen by 82%, the skylark population by 52%, and the lapwing by 52% in just eleven years – but all are doing well on this farmed area of Breckland.

The bird that gives Chris Knights the most pride is the stone curlew, or Norfolk plover, and he has the highest density of stone curlews in the country. As the population of this remarkable bird has crashed elsewhere, so numbers are still rising among his carrots, parsnips and onions. Probably the most famous photograph Chris has taken is of a stone curlew threatening a lamb – a big lamb. He was making a television film on stone curlews for Anglia Television – in the days when it still made worthwhile wildlife programmes. He ploughed up three or four acres of grass, in a field of grazing sheep, hoping to attract stone curlews. Sure enough a stone curlew came and nested so he erected a hide. Normally the sheep and stone curlews take no notice of one another, but on this occasion a ewe and three lambs came over – so the stone curlew stood up to them and saw them off.

The Chris Knights' method of farming for wildlife is simple, common sense. As a shooting man he knows that to get good populations of pheasants and partridges, a variety of habitats around the edges of the fields and along farm tracks, are required to provide food, shelter and breeding sites. These same simple needs are required for the wild birds and animals as well, conservation is as simple, or as difficult as that.

As a consequence, wild corners are left and grass or wildflowers (weeds) are encouraged around the edges of many fields, and some strips of wild bird cover are even planted. In the autumn it is possible to see another simple farming twist that could easily be followed by most farmers. Chris Knights does not cut his hedges each year (except where road safety is involved), and though he

OPPOSITE: *A stone curlew defending her nest from a lamb.*

ABOVE: *A hawthorn hedge full of berries for the birds.*
OPPOSITE: *Rule one of coastal bird photography – know your tides.*

does manage them, he will not cut until the birds have eaten the hedgerow harvest. Consequently his autumn hedges are full of hips, haws, sloes and blackberries and the hedge-cutter will only emerge when all the berries have disappeared and the birds have eaten well.

Chris Knights has been a leader of farmland conservation, but because he has led, there has also been trial and error, success and failure which have, over the years, developed into a tried and tested partnership between wildlife and farming. It has been the same in photography too; the photographs in this book show of the successes and the photograph opposite, when the tide really did turn – shows that there can still be some hiccups.

The farming of Chris Knights has been a wonderful example to both farmers and conservationists. Similarly his interest in shooting has also reinforced the very real links between shooting and conservation. For several years, as Vice-Chairman of the Countryside Restoration Trust he has tried to further the cause of practical farming and practical conservation. I hope the stunning photographs in this book do credit to an exceptional and gifted countryman.

ROBIN PAGE

CHAPTER ONE

The Farm in Summer

Whatever season of the year, the farm always has birds and wildlife. I suppose I must start with summer for that is when we have our nesting birds. We have some of the rarest and most important birds of farmland in the country. The stone curlews arrive back in the spring – at the beginning of March – together with lapwings and ringed plovers – all ground-nesting birds. I will usually see two or three pairs of stone curlews in early March – that probably means that there are another dozen pairs that I do not see.

I have been interested in stone curlews for years, and this has always been a stone curlew farm. Originally we had six to eight pairs every summer; then we took on another block of land and stone curlew numbers went up, and have continued to go up. Their numbers have risen because we have looked after them since the 1960s. At one time I assumed that they liked large open fields, but that is not so; I have found stone curlews nesting within two yards of a hedge. They also like small fields and small pieces of game cover; they even like the set-aside strips of four or five acres. In addition I have found them nesting in a narrow strip of maize – 20 yards wide. The Royal Society for the Protection of Birds (RSPB) joined in the work in the late 1980s and they have put a lot of time and money into protecting stone curlews. They are doing a great job. If we were to lose the stone curlews now, they would probably be lost for ever and we would never get them back; so we must look after them. In our area we have about 40 pairs, which is one of the highest densities in the country.

For me, one of the great appeals is that the stone curlew is a real Norfolk bird and I grew up with it – the Norfolk plover or 'thick knee'. I got to know its habitat and behaviour very well; when I worked in the fields I always made a point of finding the nests, and I have been finding them since the early 1960s – to make sure that we don't damage or disturb them. I used to chop out sugar beet with a hoe and once found a nest in a beet field. I went and told the gang, but even

OPPOSITE: *A gang of swifts – a real part of summer.*

so one man did not see the eggs and he put his feet right in the middle of them. They are so well camouflaged it was a disaster. But surprisingly they soon nested again; they are very resilient birds. They will persevere until they raise a brood. In the past, when there has been one stone curlew on a field, we have left a 20 yard square around it – like a large nest box. But we have had some fields where we have had a stone curlew's nest, then there have been several pairs of lapwings and oystercatchers join them, so, what was meant to be early parsnips, turned out to be the last field we drilled because we had to let the birds finish first. Even that can be difficult, because once all the eggs have hatched, some birds have started to lay again before we have arrived with the plough.

We have altered our farming schedule in a number of cases to suit the stone curlews, so we have put ourselves out and it has cost us money, but it has been worth it. Now, under a new agreement, we have actually received a cheque from English Nature for two pieces of barley that we sprayed off for the stone curlews. That is the first time we have received such a payment. The money side is totally unimportant to me – I just want to keep the birds. We now get a small payment for controlling predators – particularly foxes, crows and magpies. This is very important too – for the first time the Government's conservation arm has admitted the damage being done to ground-nesting birds by our booming population of predators. I like the photograph of one of our successful stone curlew's nests as it is so typical of the birds on our farm.

The ringed plovers, lapwings and oystercatchers all like the same habitat as stone curlews. With us it is large open fields, with quite a lot of stones and flints in the soil, which is typical of Breckland. They like carrot fields or fallow fields. Ringed plovers have been here for hundreds of years I suspect, although they have never been numerous. In W.G. Clarke's famous old book on the Breckland, *In Breckland Wilds*, he talks about ringed plovers. The Brecks once consisted of vast open tracts of heathland and sheep walks, and the old boys used to call the ringed plovers *stone-runners* because their legs went twinkling along over the stones; *stone-runners* – the name suits them perfectly. We never have a great number, between three and five pairs a year, but they can be double brooded. We even had little-ringed plovers' nests in a carrot field one year.

There is so much disturbance on the coast in the summer now that the few ringed plovers we have are important. Oystercatchers and shellduck have moved in from the coast because they get more peace here. We also have between 50 and 60 pairs of lapwings now: considering the way numbers are tumbling they are very important. The nests are easy to spot and so we look after them, and as a result numbers have risen dramatically over recent years. We do have one problem though: stone curlews will eat small lapwing chicks. One of our men was spraying last year and saw a stone curlew eat a ringed plover, two or three days old; it then ran up the field and ate another

OPPOSITE: *A stone curlew and chick – a successful nest.*

one. They will eat small birds if they catch them unawares; as well as earthworms, 'rainbeetles', earwigs, and 'bluebottles' – anything. The stone curlews and ringed plovers like the pieces of heathland we leave and they will nest on them if they can find a place that suits them. We keep a number of small chunks of old heath, but since the rabbits have gone, very few pieces suit the ground-nesting birds, as they preferred the heathland grazed.

We have a fine old sheep drove crossing the farm, and it must be hundreds of years old. We have tracks and droves criss-crossing the whole farm. We always say that the Breckland has one of the poorest types of soil in the country. So if we can afford to keep tracks on our land, why do the Fenmen plough their good soil right up to the dyke-edge claiming that they 'can't afford to miss a foot'?

I am so pleased that we have swallows which have always been traditional birds of farmland and farmyards. We still have two pairs in the garage and two in the out-buildings. The most important thing for them is food, and through the village there is a small river that creates

Ringed plover – 'stone-runner' and chicks.

ABOVE: *Traditional Breckland heath.*
RIGHT: *A swallow collecting mud for nest building.*

boggy patches for insects; I think that is why we have a good population of swallows, and house martins, because we still have plenty of insects for food. We put water down for them as well, in a muddy pool, so that they have nesting material; I keep it the right texture by running the vehicle through it almost every day. It is critical to provide mud for them if the spring and summer are dry.

Swallows roosting in the reeds on migration.

We still have swifts in the village too, because several of the houses have old Norfolk pantiles that are just right for nesting swifts; there are usually eight or nine pairs. To me, summer has really arrived when you can hear the swifts screaming up and down the village. They are one of the last summer migrants to arrive, and one of the first to leave. They have usually gone by 20 August and for me that means that summer is over. Some of the little screaming gangs are last year's young; they are tearaways – non-breeders getting the feel of territory. They spend all night and day on the wing – these non-breeders – incredible birds. I have seen swallows and house martins in Africa in very large numbers – but strangely I have never seen a European swift. I hope to be lucky one day.

Gilbert White, the famous old naturalist vicar summed up the beauty and the mystery of the swift – in fact he summed up the season, and one of his poems could still apply to parts of this farm:

RIGHT: *The goldfinch – King Harry.*

When day declining sheds a milder gleam,
What time the mayfly haunts the pool or stream;
When the still owl skims round the grassy mead,
What time the limorous hare limps forth to feed;
Then be the time to steal adown the vale,
And listen to the vagrant cuckoo's tale,
To hear the clamorous curlew call his mate:
Or the soft quail his tender pain relate;
To see the swallow sweep the dark'ning plain
Belated, to support her infant train;
To mark the swift in rapid giddy ring
Dash round the steeple, unsubdued of wing:
Amusive Birds! – say where your hid retreat
When the frost rages and the tempests beat;
Whence your return, by such nice instinct led;
When spring, soft season, lifts her bloomy head?
Such baffled searches mock men's prying pride.
The God of Nature is your secret guide.

The picture of the little gang flying (see page 18) was not easy to take. However, it is much easier trying to take photographs of flying swifts today, with modern cameras and the technology of auto-focus and fast films. It is still quite tricky and requires patience, but it is much easier than it was in the 1960s.

Goldfinches have done very well in the last few years, and they nest in the garden in pear trees, apple trees and the garden walls. The old people in the village used to call them King Harry's – because of the gold on the wings and brilliant red faces. The nest, if they've got young, is a very messy affair, as their bills are not suitable to clear the nest of droppings. The nest is made of reeds and fine grasses with bits of moss; it is quite a coarse structure compared with some of the other nests. We get quite a lot of goldfinches in the autumn and winter. On pieces of land where we have had vegetable crops the groundsel comes up in the autumn and we get large flocks – some with over 100 birds. Now and again we get 150 at the back of the house on some rough ground. They are beautiful birds and always worth seeing. The goldfinch is one of the few birds that is now doing very well (up 10%). Suddenly, it seems, they have discovered bird-feeders and so soon they may start doing even better.

Blue tits are well established peanut-eaters of course, and are also flourishing. They come to our bird-feeders but there are not as many as there were. We only have two or three pairs now –

A blue tit having a wash and brush up.

compared to a dozen a few years ago. It was good to see them on the nuts – but then the sparrowhawks found them. We have more coal tits than blue tits now. I took this attractive picture from a hide. Terry Andrewartha and I made a little drinking pool for birds, but this little blue tit decided to have a wash and brush-up before sunning itself to dry off. All the tit family like to do this if they get the chance.

We still have yellowhammers in quite good numbers. They like the grassy banks all over the farm, and they will nest in low vegetation, in grass or bracken, very low down, and sometimes on the ground. We see them throughout the year and we get mini flocks later in the autumn and winter. They seem to prefer nesting where there is a piece of set-aside next to a hedge and where it is quiet. I have found one or two nests in set-aside in front of hedges and banks and so we keep the machinery away from it. In general, numbers have decreased, but we seem to have a stable population.

LEFT: *A yellowhammer foraging for food.*
BELOW: *Flowers and seeds left for the birds.*

House sparrows were once in large numbers on every farm.

I always hesitate when people talk about plummeting bird numbers – what do they expect? Before and after the Second World War we had no sparrowhawks and it was legal to control them. Now they are back – you can't have large numbers of small birds and sparrowhawks. There are signs that sparrowhawk numbers have peaked – they may have cleaned out their own food supply; it will be interesting to see what happens.

Thomas Bewick had mixed feelings about the sparrowhawk: '*The sparrowhawk is very numerous in various parts of the world, from Russia to the Cape of Good Hope. It is a bold and spirited bird; but is obedient and docile, and can be easily trained to hunt Partridge and Quails; it makes great destruction among pigeons, young poultry and small birds of all kinds, which it will attack and carry off in the most daring manner.*'

I suppose sparrowhawks got their name from hunting sparrows. We once had large flocks of sparrows, but now we only have about 30 to 40 coming to the bird-feeders. They have to come as there are no bullock yards in the village any more, in fact there are no cattle at all. There used to be four or five dairy herds with yards of bullocks, but they have all disappeared. That means important food sources for finches and sparrows have all gone. EU regulations have not helped, as all corn has to be stored in bird-proof buildings, and so there is not the food on farms any more for the large flocks. I think, and hope, that sparrows are very resilient birds and they will overcome this problem and make a comeback in due course. It would be good to have them in the fields again at harvest time. I feed them all the year round in the garden with corn, and numbers are holding up well. They are chirpy little birds, especially when you get 10 or 20 of them in a bush all chirping away. It

takes me back years to when numbers were high. They use my peanut feeders, as well as the sunflower feeders and I put mixed grain down for them. It is amusing in late summer when the young have left the nest and they are as large as the adults. They sit around begging, with their wings quivering; it reminds me of some teenage children doing the same thing. I don't think sparrows make up very much of the sparrowhawks' prey these days; it seems to prefer more exotic meals – turtle doves, swallows, wrens, mistle thrushes and blackbirds.

I would love to have corn buntings on the farm, but for some reason we don't get them and we seem unable to attract them. Perhaps the ground is not flat enough or there are too many hedges and trees. The stronghold for them is in the Fens – Ten Mile Bank, Spalding and the Deepings – they seem to prefer wide open spaces.

One of the very special summer birds is the yellow wagtail. We get a few pairs attempt to nest each spring in the water meadows and grass fields. The photograph here was taken on a friend's farm, on a piece of organic land, where he had them nesting. The picture was taken from a hide, when the adults were

ABOVE: *House sparrows gleaning the stubble.*
LEFT: *A corn bunting on its song perch.*
RIGHT: *A yellow wagtail with food for its young.*

feeding their brood. In the spring they love running around cattle – they look like little golden guineas flitting about. I was lucky enough to be at Rutland Water one day when there was a big passage of yellow wagtails going through and pausing to feed around the cattle. There were between 10 and 15 birds round each animal and it was such a treat to see them – they are lovely birds.

The nightingale is another lovely summer bird and we get them in two or three places. We have a large wood and we get anything up to 10 to 12 pairs singing in there. They are such beautiful songsters. A lot of birds seem to be declining and many of the experts blame modern farming, but look at the birds we have here. I wonder if the decline in migrants is caused by the Sahara Desert getting larger. If you fly over it in a plane it seems immense; so what it means to some of our summer visitors I cannot imagine – their journeys are both incredible and dangerous. So, if the desert

keeps expanding it might mean that we lose even more of our migrants. The nightingale is very special to the English countryside and we are still very fortunate to have it. I love to go round in the evening and hear it sing.

This picture was taken on one such evening from my vehicle. When my brother lived near King's Lynn he had a nightingale start singing just outside his house. The first night it was wonderful: within a week he was complaining that it was singing all night and keeping him awake: 'I am going to shoot that bloody nightingale,' he muttered. I am glad to say that he never carried out his threat.

I think the poet Robert Bridges would have disagreed with my brother.

Beautiful must be the mountains whence ye come,
And bright in the fruitful valleys the streams, wherefrom
Ye learn your song:
Where are those starry woods? O might I wander there,
Among the flowers, which in that heavenly air
Bloom the year long!

Nay, barren are those mountains and spent the streams:
Our song is the voice of desire, that haunts our dreams,
A throe of the heart,

The nightingale a plain little bird with a 'bootiful' song.

Whose pining visions dim, forbidden hopes profound,
No dying cadence nor long sigh can sound,
For all our art.

Alone, aloud in the raptured ear of men
We pour our dark nocturnal secret; and then,
As night is withdrawn
From these sweet-springing meads and bursting boughs of May,
Dream, while the innumerable choir of day
Welcome the dawn.

Turtle doves are most attractive birds that have seen a sharp decrease in numbers over recent years. Fortunately, after a very lean spell all through the 1990s, we have suddenly started seeing a few more and I hope it is a trend that continues. Years ago I would ring them. There would be four

A turtle dove – still shot in France.

or five in the cage every morning. I had several recoveries from Portugal and Spain – shot – which is a great shame. To hear a turtle dove almost purring away is a wonderful summer sound – it really is magic. Sadly we have had stone curlews' rings back too – shot in France. They are protected there too, but our continental cousins seem to regard us as stone curlew gamekeepers. They are either law-breakers – or they are useless at identifying birds. Whatever their excuse, they should not be shooting stone curlews.

The picture of the young cuckoo was taken in the garden – in a gooseberry bush; its foster-mother is a hedge sparrow. Around here the nests of hedge sparrows and pied wagtails are the ones most favoured by cuckoos. Further afield, the favourite nest belongs to the reed war-bler. We still do hear cuckoos, but not in the numbers we did once. Their decline is very sad as their call is a real part of the countryside. I wonder, again, if the prob-lem is caused by their long migration.

Fortunately, one bird is still very com-mon in the Breckland – the pheasant. It is the pheasant that has made the Breckland as it is today. The early Victorians built country houses, and there were estates from 5000 acres to 20,000 acres which

LEFT: *A hedge sparrow feeding a young cuckoo.*
RIGHT: *The pheasant – so important to the economy and wildlife habitats of Norfolk.*

were run almost exclusively for shooting. They planted woods, belts of trees and coverts, and so it is an inheritance that the pheasant has given us; a sort of bio-diversity of countryside based on the pheasant. If those early landowners had not been keen on sport, or on making more money to keep their estates going there would have been vast tracts of open countryside totally lacking in woods and coverts – woods planted so that the pheasant could be driven out and shot at. I approve of shooting; but if you go out to shoot pheasants – then you should shoot pheasants, not woodcock and everything else. Pheasants have done more for keeping a greater number of birds in the countryside than anything else.

If you want to find wildlife nowadays, you have to go where there is a shoot and where there is a gamekeeper. Shooting with a keeper means that there is good habitat, food and protection, because of sensible predator control. The work of a keeper is very similar to that of a wildlife warden. Where there is no shooting – there is no wildlife, and where there is shooting – there is wildlife, it is as simple and as obvious as that. Small birds like game cover crops and they provide plenty of food.

I shoot, and I enjoy it; there is a close link between country sports and conservation – but I'd rather go taking photographs. The great thing about shooting is not necessarily the actual shooting – it is meeting like-minded people. You meet with country people and you hear stories about woodcock, hares, foxes and all sorts of birds – it really is country talk. It is not quite a gossip club – but very close to it. It is a day spent in the fields and woods with friends. I am a very moderate type of shooter, but I have to say that I enjoy eating pheasants as well as photographing them. I have to say too that we do have a gamekeeper – a very good one. If we didn't we would lose a tremendous number of birds. I am not talking just of pheasants and partridges here – I am referring to stone curlews, lapwings, common curlews and all the ground-nesting birds, including the grey partridges. Stoats, foxes and carrion crows are the three main predators.

Magpies are important predators too and we control them. They are attractive and clever birds, but there are too many of them. We never used to have any in this part of the world, but they are getting more and more common; they will take eggs, and small birds just out of the nest. They sit and spy out the land always watching; they will see a song thrush feeding its chicks, then, when the adult leaves, the magpie is down and eating its young. A lot of professional conservationists seem to have lost touch with the real countryside; they have done college courses in environmental studies but have never lived in or done practical work in the countryside. You have to experience nature at first hand: then you will see magpies clearing out nests. You will never get rid of the last magpie so they should be controlled for the sake of vulnerable and rare species.

RIGHT: *A curlew and chicks – very vulnerable to predators.*

The magpie – a clever and destructive predator.

I saw carrion crows attacking a leveret in a field one day, and then the old hare came. She drew them off, 40 yards away, and then chased them another 40 yards. In the end they sat in the hedge and the young leveret got into better cover. When you work on the land you see these things; sitting over a book of environmental studies you would never learn that carrion crows would attack something as large as a leveret. It was an eye opener for me. I have also seen carrion crows take toad after toad at spawning time, and moorhens' eggs. I've watched them bury what they have taken and come back for more. So magpies and carrion crows are the pirates of the bird world, but they are very clever. Fewer keepers mean more magpies. Unfortunately modern life has made the magpie too successful. It feeds from bird tables; it finds food on livestock farms; it finds young garden birds easy prey and it feeds all the year round on the birds and animals killed in millions on our roads.

Although this book is about the birds that have given me so much pleasure, I have to say that the way we farm is also good for animals, we have a thriving hare population and I love to see them. We have always had lots of hares, and they like set-aside and the winter vegetable crops we grow. We leave winter stubbles for them and the hares lay up in them all winter. Hares will breed for 10 months of the year and I have found leverets in January and February. Terry Andrewartha filmed a hare with leverets just born – still wet. She had four leverets all together, then, when they dried off, they moved away to spread out. I have seen the young come back in the evening and the doe suckles them two or three at a time, she doesn't hide them. They just spread out and split up naturally – it is one way to reduce the risk of predation. Sometimes hares damage trees and crops and so some limited control is needed. I do not intend to be controversial here – but in my view it is much more humane to kill a hare with a dog – coursing – than with a gun. With a dog, the hare is either caught and killed, or it gets away. Hare shoots are dreadful – with hares

RIGHT AND BELOW: *The brown hare is thriving on 'conservation' farms.*

being wounded and maimed, and how they scream. I do not like hare shoots on my farm, and I do not go on hare shoots. It is back to practical experience again – it is humane control with a greyhound or lurcher – and inhumane control with a gun and political correctness.

We have other animals; stoats, weasels and roe deer. We control them – but the emphasis is on control not extermination. I have to admit that I did not take the dormouse picture on the farm – although I would very much like to have them here if we had the right habitat.

In the 1970s I made a film on roe deer, with Terry. It was wonderful to do. There were very few on farmland then and virtually all our filming was around Thetford Chase. Now, with 'clear felling', the roe deer have spread out and there has been a population explosion. They have spread out and we have them all over the farm. The does often have twins and there is a dominant buck in charge of each territory. They do not do all that much damage and they are very beautiful to watch.

Barn owls are beautiful to watch too and we are lucky to have so many. I am really pleased with the picture of the

LEFT: *The weasel is an attractive little predator.*
RIGHT: *The secretive dormouse.*

ABOVE: *Roe deer at dawn.*
LEFT: *A little owl at dusk.*
RIGHT: *Barn owl chicks almost ready to leave the nest.*

hunting 'white owl' (see the frontispiece). It hunts regularly over the same piece of ground. Every evening it was hunting in the same place, at the same time, so one evening I just set up the camera and it came past right on cue. It was as easy as that.

We have other owls in addition to the barn owl. We have two or three pairs of little owls most years. The picture of the little owl at sunset is totally genuine. The nest was in an old tree close by. Ninety per cent of their prey is earthworms taken in the evening; even when it has not been raining they rush

about and sometimes they will bring in a beetle or a small mouse. The male presents the mouse to the female, not the chicks. You see all these things when you are in a hide – you learn so much more than simply reading a text book.

We get short-eared owls too, several spend the wintertime here. They roost in old pit holes, hawthorn bushes and hedgerows. They are big owls and they fly up and down in late afternoon over the heaths, grass tracks and stubble fields. They are powerful birds. I took this picture by driving along carefully, it was sitting on a fence post, and I came to within 20 yards of it.

The other great predator on the farm is the sparrowhawk. It sits on top of the food chain around here. I never used to see them at all, now we see them all the time and they wreak havoc with small birds especially round bird-feeders. They are doing this all the year throughout the whole countryside. A pair of sparrowhawks need a couple of thousand small birds a year to live on and raise a family. This one has spread itself out to protect the chicks from a thunder storm. I like to see them, but you do not want too many of them. I think numbers will sort themselves out in due course. They have no predators themselves and so I think you should be allowed to control them. Up to the First World War you were allowed to shoot them, and there were still plenty about. It was insecticides that killed them in huge numbers, that was terrible. But when the chemicals causing the trouble were banned, they came back very strongly. It seems to me that if they were put back on the shooting list there would still be some about, as they are very secretive birds and they would become a lot more wary – but it would do several other species a lot of good if there were fewer sparrowhawks. Wildlife is under threat from everything – sparrowhawks, motor cars, pollution, and farming. We are lucky to have as much wildlife as we have.

Kingfishers breed on the farm and there is a small population throughout the Breckland. Because of the mild winters they have been doing quite well. I was photographing a

LEFT: *A short-eared owl on watch.*
RIGHT: *A sparrowhawk sheltering her young from the rain.*

kingfisher on a nearby estate when the game-keeper said to me: 'I am sorry that that first nest did not come to anything, I have not seen them going in and out for a while, but don't worry it has nested again immediately behind it. However I haven't seen the female. The male is feeding that nest.' I sat there. The male came up and took a fish in and fed the young. Then the next time the male came up there was another kingfisher that came with it and settled on the branch – that was a large youngster begging food; the male went into the hole. Then the female came up and fed the one that could fly, I thought that one was from a first brood. So they were feeding *the first brood, and the second brood* and then I saw a third hole, and she was sitting on a clutch of eggs as well. Kingfishers are relatively easy to film when they are nesting, and if a perch is provided they will sit on it – hence all the photographs with a kingfisher sitting on a 'No Fishing' sign. They have usually been erected especially for the photograph.

I could not resist including the next two pictures. Golden orioles do not nest on the farm but they do nest close by. They are rare as nesting birds in Britain as we are on the very edge of their range. They are quite common in France and Spain. Their song is as beautiful as their plumage and so it is one of the most spectacular birds we have. They like to nest in poplars in the Fens. Some years there are quite a few nests and in others there are none.

TOP: *A kingfisher takes a rest from feeding three broods of young.*
LEFT: *The golden oriole will hopefully become better established here.*

A pair of golden oriole feeding their hungry brood.

There is a golden oriole group who wanted some photographs. The young do not stay in the nest long and so we hadn't much time. Because they nest so high up, 50 feet, we had permission to photograph and use a mechanical cherry picker. I went up with Terry to have a look – before we had put a hide on it. Much to our amazement the bird came and fed the chicks anyway, taking absolutely no notice of us – so we just took the photographs where we were.

It would be wonderful to get more of them nesting all over East Anglia.

CHAPTER TWO

The Farm in Winter

I like the winter. Harvest is out of the way but with vegetables the season actually makes very little difference; the work load is the same the whole year round. But winter here is always very special because of the abundant wildlife. It is strange, in the summer I am always looking forward to the winter, and in the winter, I am looking forward to the spring and summer. I really do enjoy every season – in fact I enjoy every day as it comes. The winter in Breckland is just as exceptional and exciting as the summertime. The plough brings in the birds, and it really is a case of the feather and the furrow. They chase after all the earthworms and other beetles and bugs, and the invertebrates that the plough turns up. When you get well into the winter, great flocks of lapwings join the seagulls and it makes a wonderful spectacle. Our home-grown lapwings move on

into Spain and France, but we host the Scandinavian birds by the thousand. You see large flocks of them sharing the fields with golden plovers; it makes a wonderful scene. They have their favourite fields they go to, and being a little inland we get masses and masses of golden plovers. They are beautiful birds. It seems as if they almost hear the tractor start, for as soon as the ploughing begins, they appear. The plough travels much faster now than in the old days and so they have to make the best of it. We still have plenty of earthworms and life in the soil which is good for

OPPOSITE: *Pink-footed geese flying across the full moon at dawn.*

RIGHT: *Gulls and plovers following the plough.*

A rainbow in early autumn.

the birds. The lapwings nest in March, by the time it is June they are in small flocks all seeming to go west – I don't know where they go at that time, but our summer population goes to northern Spain in the winter, and we get birds from Denmark and Scandinavia. We get vast flocks of them.

We are very low lying here, about 50 feet above sea level, which means big open skies which can be spectacular at any season of the year. The picture of the rainbow was taken on a local farm in early autumn, and gives you an idea of the wonderful sky-scapes we see. Farm tracks criss-cross the whole area and are very important for wildlife, providing food, cover and breeding sites. I took the photograph of this track just as the catkins were coming out and it looked most attractive. All over East Anglia there are green tracks where people can walk; most of them very old, and some are ancient drove roads. We probably don't need all these tracks; or at least they need to be rationalised. We had a nice track around two sides of a field here, but ramblers insisted on a footpath diagonally across the field. It was a much nicer walk around the edges, under the hedges, than straight across a

One of the many tracks criss-crossing the Breckland.

50-acre muddy field. Political correctness is a strange ailment – particularly when the end result is a worse walk. The tracks are important for wildlife because the grass is kept shorter and the birds and rodents can find seeds from flowers and trees on the ground; pheasants and pigeons love these areas for feeding. Small seeds such as hornbeam, and even larger ones such as acorns are not so easy to find in long grass. Earthworms are not just found in the fields and these old tracks are full of worms; if you walk up them after dark you will often find the short grass covered with them. Some surprising birds love these tracks at night to wine and dine on worms – stone curlews and little owls are regulars. Many animals too regard worms as delicacies, and both foxes and badgers love them.

The rivers in this part of the country are very important as the Breckland is notoriously dry. Every so often there are little breaks in the chalk, giving rise to clear running streams through the whole area. The picture of the Gadder (see page 53) is only about a mile from where it rises out of the chalk; two or three miles further on it becomes quite a large stream and flows into the Wissey and then the Great Ouse. From there it flows on to King's Lynn and out into the Wash. The Nar is in the northern part of Breckland, as are the Gadder, the Wissey, and the Lark. The contours around the Gadder seem to roll down into a little valley which still has water meadows on each side: the water meadows are very important for hunting barn owls, feeding lapwings. Redshank like them too.

Jack snipe come in the autumn, they are smaller then the common snipe, and because of this they are known as 'the half snipe' in Norfolk. They nest in the Finnish forests and when ordinary snipe are displaying they make the famous 'drumming' noise, but the jack snipe sounds more like a horse galloping into the distance, 'Clip cloppetty, clip cloppety'. Jack snipe are usually seen in the winter. The main difference between the common snipe and the jack snipe is simple; the jack snipe is slightly smaller with a shorter bill, the common snipe also has a straight line down the centre of the crown where the jack snipe doesn't. When flushed, jack snipe don't call, they fly up suddenly and

OPPOSITE: *The River Gadder close to its source.*
BELOW: *Jack snipe, known as 'the half snipe' in Norfolk.*

drop down again only about 20 yards further on; common snipe give a sort of whispy call and fly off at great high speed, twisting and diving. The common snipe flies fast, that is why it was once prized by shooting men. Thomas Bewick, the old naturalist and wood engraver wrote *'When first disturbed, it utters a kind of feeble whistle, and generally flies against the wind, turning nimbly in a zigzag direction for two or three hundred paces, and sometimes soaring almost out of sight... From its vigilance and manner of flying, it is one of the most difficult birds to shoot. Some sportsmen can imitate their cries, and by that means*

draw them within reach of their shoot: others, of a less honourable description, prefer the more certain method of catching them in the night by a spring like that which is used for the woodcock.'

Sadly snipe numbers are plummeting; they have declined by 90% in twenty-five years because of habitat loss and predation. They are much too beautiful to shoot in my opinion. We don't get many jack snipe, but we were in a stubble field one day and out of the middle of nowhere a jack snipe got up – the last place I would ever expect to find one. They are usually near marshy, boggy ground. They are pretty little birds.

The streams are important for herons too; they have good populations of small fish and so the herons find them important. We tend to take herons for granted, but they are very attractive birds with remarkable yellow eyes. Their beaks are sharp and can be quite dangerous. In my bird ringing days there was a chap cycling down the road with a heron under his arm. As soon as I came up to him it pecked me on the hand; it hurt, and I was lucky I wasn't pecked in an eye. The bird was injured, but recovered alright as they are quite tough.

A heron – with beautiful yellow eyes, but a sharp and dangerous beak.

In the early days – when I was a bit slimmer, in the 1960s – we would climb up to herons' nests to ring the young. It was quite frightening because the nests were very high. The local names for the heron vary from 'harnser' to 'frank', for its call, to 'heronshaw'.

A lot of my interest in birds grew from ringing. I finished up ringing lapwings, turtle doves and stone curlews, mainly to find out where they spent their winters. I had several recoveries from France and Portugal; unfortunately some had been shot. I don't ring anymore and I think there is too much ringing for the sake of ringing. Ringing should take place to increase our knowledge; it should not be regarded as a hobby.

Farm hedges and domestic gardens are very important in winter for a variety of birds.

The pictures of the mistle thrush and the song thrush were taken on the same holly tree just before Christmas. The mistle thrush is a very special bird. It starts singing earlier than the other birds – showing that winter will soon be turning to spring. This picture was taken as the hawthorn berries had almost been cleared up, and the holly berries were the only ones left.

A mistle thrush on holly.

A song thrush looking for food.

Tennyson's poem of the song thrush describes the song perfectly.

The Throstle

Summer is coming, summer is coming.
I know it, I know it, I know it.
Light again, leaf again, life again, love again;
Yes, my wild little poet.

Sing the new year in under the blue
Last year you sang it as gladly
'New, new, new, new!' Is it then so new
That you should carol so madly?

'Love again, song again, nest again, young again,'
Never a prophet so crazy!
And hardly a daisy as yet, little friend,
See, there is hardly a daisy.

'Here again, here, here, here, happy year!'
O warble unchidden, unbidden!
Summer is coming, is coming, my dear,
And all the winters are hidden.

Fieldfares come in every year in large numbers and spend six or seven days with us, gorging themselves on hawthorn berries and drinking in puddles. They leave plenty of droppings around, before moving on. If the weather is hard they will clear up every last berry. They obviously prefer hawthorn berries, as they eat them first – but in a cold winter everything goes.

Around the farm we never cut the hedges until the birds have cleared all the berries. I can never understand those farmers who cut their hedges early – in late summer. Those who cut them every year I understand even less. We cut every three years, except the ones beside the road, which are trimmed more often for safety reasons. If you leave the hedges for three years you get berries, if you cut them every year you get no berries.

Redwings are attracted to the berries in hedgerows.

Redwings are other attractive winter visitors. They don't go in such large flocks as fieldfares, we usually get two or three in the garden, and they are quieter and more docile than fieldfares. They are brilliant little birds and are now breeding in northern Scotland. Most of the winter fieldfares come from Norway and Sweden, the redwings are mainly from Scandinavia too. It is nothing for them to fly over the North Sea in a single night. Flying at 30–40 miles per hour on a nice night they soon get over the North Sea. It is important for migrating birds to choose good weather.

The blackcap now often over-winters in Britain.

The picture of the blackcap is interesting. The blackcap was once thought to be a summer visitor, but now an increasing number are spending the winter here. This picture was taken on the day of a blizzard and I was photographing fieldfares on apples; suddenly the male blackcap appeared and seemed unconcerned at the adverse weather conditions. It appeared quite at home and made an excellent, but unexpected picture.

At one time it was thought that blackcaps were strictly insectivorous, but they are clearly opportunist and apples now feature on their winter diet sheet.

The mild winters we seem to have help a lot of birds and convince them to stay here, rather than to charge off to southern climes in France, Spain, Cyprus and Malta where they are likely to be shot and eaten. They have decided it is safer to stay here.

Robins do well in winter gardens and this picture has been made into a Christmas card for the Countryside Restoration Trust. With our big hedges we get plenty of robins staying out on the farmland for the whole year.

Bullfinches have always been a favourite bird of mine. Over the years I have often seen them down a lane where there are some guelder rose bushes growing to a tremendous height. I saw that the bullfinches feed on them late in winter, so I planted some in the garden. This year we have seen bullfinches coming to feed on the new bushes, so I put the hide up and the photograph overleaf resulted. When a bullfinch flies it is easy to identify because of its distinctive white rump. Bullfinches are disappearing fast; they are down 62%, so I hope my guelder roses can attract some to stay as we have some good habitat for them. Their predicament has been caused by the

A robin posing for a Christmas card.

loss of hedges and orchards and also because of predation. They seem easy targets for sparrowhawks and their young fall victim to woodpeckers and even mistle thrushes. If you see five or six bullfinches together it is a big flock and so they are very vulnerable to predation. Goldfinches, on the other hand, come in much larger flocks and so there are always birds on the lookout. We get as many as 150 goldfinches on our sunflower heads. Goldfinches have recently started to use garden peanuts from feeders and somehow the message is spreading throughout the county.

ABOVE: *The bullfinch – a bird in decline.*
RIGHT: *The goldfinch – one of the few farmland birds doing well.*

Long-tailed tits come through about once a week – but I have never found a nest in the garden. They move about in family parties during the winter. The long-tailed tit is another bird which discovered peanuts four or five years ago. My sister has had 27 on her feeders at one time – is that a record? They are nice to watch when there is a whole gang of them. They are nice to listen to as well with their twittering calls; they keep calling as if they are worried that they will get left behind.

We are lucky as we still get tree sparrows coming into the garden. We have two little flocks on the farm and we try to ensure they have plenty of food. I believe that there are more about than people think, but they just don't notice them. The Game Conservancy at Loddington has them; Rutland Water has them. They are much more flighty than the house sparrow. A house sparrow will fly up into a tree, but the tree sparrow will fly up and go to the other side of the field and sit in a tree. We feed them on linseed and rape seed, on the ground. Pheasants, yellowhammers and finches are all encouraged by this. In the old days much seed was spilt on the average farm – which fed the birds by accident. Now we spill it on purpose to encourage birds onto the farm.

We see treecreepers occasionally; they are very solitary little birds. They don't make a lot of calls as they don't need to communicate. They nest in cracks in tree trunks or branches or where the bark has peeled off. They are very difficult to photograph as they move so quickly. When I have the camera I have to be ready in case one comes by; they usually arrive when I am photographing something else and so it is difficult. With the one pictured overleaf, I was trying to take some great tits at a feeding place and the treecreeper came

LEFT: *Long-tailed tits – doing well on winter peanuts.*
RIGHT: *The tree sparrow – still on the farm.*

on the next tree. They are superb little birds, with a fine long curved bill for getting insects and spiders out of the crevices in the bark.

It is always a bonus to see a barn owl – winter or summer. I often see them in winter, even in day time. I have watched them in the morning hunting for voles; they will be out all day after a wet and windy night. I have seen as many as four in one field, it was a marvellous sight. We have a very good population at the moment. We put nest boxes up for them, but they prefer natural sites. First choice is a hole in a tree, then a ledge in a barn or bale stack. Then they will try a nest box. I had nest boxes up for 8 years; but they were up for 6 years before they were used, the barn owls preferring a barn and then an ash tree. A tawny owl took over the nest in the ash tree; the displaced owls then pushed the pair out of the barn, so they had to go back into a nest box. In the three parishes near us, there must be nine or ten pairs of barn owls. The way we farm and leave rough areas allows the small rodents to breed which are essential for barn owls. In the old days the 'white owl' was also associated with churches – hence Tennyson's 'The Owl';

> When cats run home and light is come
> And dew is cold upon the ground,
> And the far-off stream is dumb,
> And the whirring sail goes round
> and the whirring sail goes round;
> Alone and warming his five wits,
> The white owl in the belfry sits.
>
> When merry milkmaid click the latch,
> And rarely smells the new-mown hay,
> And the cock hath sung beneath the thatch
> Twice or thrice his roundelay
> Twice or thrice his roundelay;
> Alone and warming his five wits
> The white owl in the belfry sits.

ABOVE: *A treecreeper –*
a secretive little bird.
RIGHT: *A barn owl*
looking for prey.

Grey partridges cope very well in winter if they have some cover. Nationally, numbers have gone down a lot, but in some places they are holding their own and doing quite well. I think they are superb little birds of farmland – really part of the English countryside, like the barn owl. They are certainly in the premier division of birds. French partridges are attractive birds, but are very different from the grey. The grey, or English, lays more eggs than any other bird in the northern hemisphere, 22 or 23. They hatch all together, and she tucks the egg shells into each other to take less room. As she talks to the chicks, the cock bird comes and sits beside her and keeps taking the chicks from her as they hatch; they are working in perfect harmony as a pair. The French builds a nest, lays eggs, covers them up and forgets about them, they are not the brightest of birds (typically French). They then go off and build another one. I haven't seen it, but some say that the male will sit on one nest and the female on the other. So they have two single-parented nests.

The end of winter is signalled by the pheasants fighting. By the time you get to mid-March the cocks are really sparring and showing off to the hen birds. Each cock can look after seven or eight hens. Ones which are dominant will collect their harem of hen birds, and the loser will just go and fight the next one. They fight so much that they can be in a pretty poor state by the end of the season. It is marvellous to see them when they are displaying; they put one wing down, and one wing up, and spread out their tail so that it matches the wing, and then they run round the hen, really

LEFT: *A red-legged or French partridge.*
RIGHT: *A grey or English partridge.*

showing off. All pheasants display, I've seen a peacock pheasant showing off with its wings, and its tail spread out nearly to the size of an armchair, it was fantastic.

For this picture I saw the fight developing and was ready with my camera. I took a series of pictures from the vehicle, it was a good job I was comfortable as the battle lasted a long time with any number of skirmishes. Normally fighting cocks see you and keep one eye on you, and the other on the other bird. By doing this they gradually move sideways away from you, but this pair took no notice of me and kept fighting. I used a 500mm lens with 1.4 converter, the equivalent of a 700mm lens.

Geese are a real feature of the farm and the whole area in winter. A lot have gone by the middle of March, with only the remnants left. They are long distance flyers and have been known to pop across to Lancashire (Southport and along the coast) if we get a hard snap here. After two or three days if the weather has turned, they come back to Norfolk. The picture on page 48 is of pinkfeet as they flew perfectly in front of the moon. Pinkfeet have done very well: a few years ago there were only about 70,000–80,000, but we get that number in Norfolk alone now. The total population is probably around 220,000. The increase has arisen because of mild winters; they have also learnt to feed off the farmland more – eating the shoots of winter wheat and the tops of carrots and sugar beet after they have been harvested. Because of the better feeding it means that they arrive at their breeding grounds in much better condition. They breed in the Spitzbergen area and because they are in better condition they have larger broods. Some farmers in north Norfolk deliberately leave their sugar beet tops for the geese. I think they should have a special payment for doing this: it is good for conservation and it is good for tourism – a lot of people come to see the geese in winter – it is a spectacular sight.

One of my favourite times is to get up in the winter before dawn and photograph geese coming in on the sunrise. It is magical – you sit in the darkness and then hear the first pinkfeet coming in. It is always a thrill. The pinkfeet picture on page 48 is totally genuine: geese on a full moon at dawn. It was a close run thing – the pinkfeet, or the pheasants, for the cover of the book. The pheasants won.

LEFT: *Cock pheasants fighting – spring is on the way.*

CHAPTER THREE

The Coast

The farm is 26 miles from the Wash. It means that we get many coastal birds on the farm, but I also travel to the coast to see the birds. I love the coast and go at all times of the year, visiting the Wash and moving along to Wells and Cley. There are cliffs, salt marshes and sand dunes; it has become the mecca of British bird watching along the north Norfolk coast. I have been going since I was 16, on a motorbike, and I enjoy it just as much today. The most amazing time is in winter and early spring when all the waders are back. Some of the scenes must be among the wildlife wonders of the world. I go in summer much less, as we get migratory crockles (tourists) at that time of year and they swamp the roads and beaches.

ABOVE: *Hunstanton beach and cliffs.*
OPPOSITE: *An oystercatcher in danger of losing its snack to turnstones.*

There are so many tourists, and with all the disturbance that goes with them, many of the oystercatchers and shellduck move inland because they can't find enough room on the coast.

Some people find it surprising that Hunstanton is a great place for watching birds. From the cliff tops you can watch the sea ducks in wintertime; long tailed ducks, scoter, eider, velvet scoter, and occasionally scaup. Goldeneye go to the pits at Snettersham and are very attractive. Around the rocks you get turnstone, purple sandpipers and a whole host of waders. Fulmers nest on the cliffs and by the end of February the fulmers are back on the cliffs; there is such a competition for nest sites that they are easy to see.

71

LEFT: *A typical summer scene at Morston Quay.*
BELOW: *The appropriately named common seal.*

Years ago James Fisher wrote a famous book on fulmers; the only place where they nested in the British Isles in those days was St Kilda, and now they have spread and spread. There are so many on Fair Isle that the resident peregrines had to 'push off' as the fulmers spattered them with fish oil as a means of defence. I've seen them nest in walls at the edges of fields up there, because there are so many of them.

The whole area of the north Norfolk coast is very attractive with much variety. At Morston there is an attractive little quay among the creeks and it is a favourite area of holiday-makers as well as locals. From Morston it is possible to get a boat to see the seals; they are common seals and make a

great natural tourist attraction. They have very appealing eyes and arouse the 'bunny hugger' syndrome. That is not necessarily a bad thing as long as it gets people interested in wildlife and real conservation.

Cley Marshes are a mecca for birds, and pictures of the reedbeds and windmill are well known. The rarities keep turning up there, it must be at exactly the right place where East Anglia sticks out into the North Sea. Further east there are cliffs and so the birds fly in from Scandinavia and find the low lying marshes at Cley exactly to their liking. It is so low that they are building a new sea wall now. Years ago there used to be a little port there bringing in coal for local use, but it is silted up now. They still cut reed in the marshes in the traditional way, but the windmill no longer grinds corn. There are several windmills dotted along the coast, because of the vigorous onshore and offshore winds. The best time for birds is in the autumn with the east wind blowing, bringing migrants to Blakeney Point – as a result we get a lot of rarities, such as bluethroats – which also brings in flocks of 'twitchers', sometimes by the hundred.

A lot of twitchers are very good bird-watchers and are very knowledgeable, but I do not really like the concept of twitching. If a rare bird turned up in your garden you could have 2000 twitchers outside the next day. I like rare birds, but I get just as much pleasure watching a puffin or a green woodpecker.

Some twitchers are very single minded and it seems that they do not always appreciate what

ABOVE: *Cutting reed in the traditional way at Cley.*
RIGHT: *A flock of 'twitchers'.*

ABOVE: *Brent geese in the early morning.*
LEFT: *The wind turbine at Swaffham – a new type of 'windmill'.*

they are doing or what they are looking at. They see their rare bird for a few seconds and then say: 'Good, great. I've got it', they tick their list of birds and off they go. I just do not understand that.

Just as East Anglia once had many windmills, now at Swaffham we have a new one. In the old days it was to grind corn – but this one produces electricity. It is said to produce enough for half of Swaffham's needs. Perhaps they ought to build a couple more – that would be fantastic. If this is the way forward – with no noise and no pollution – so be it. Swaffham is 100 feet higher than we are, and the wind generator is on the top of a hill. We can see it but it is not a problem as we find it quite attractive.

Geese rely on the wind too; most arrive in the autumn, in early October, and with a following wind they can cover huge distances surprisingly quickly. Pinkfeet and Brent stay longer than the others. The goose picture above is of Brent, there are more and more of them now that they are eating from the fields. I think the limiting factor for geese will not be the food here, but the food available when they travel to their breeding grounds. In the Arctic, they only get one chance of nesting,

ABOVE: *Pinkfeet on Norfolk stubble.*
LEFT: *Whitefronts at Holkham.*

and to raise their young goslings – so if they get blizzards or snow storms that year, that can be it. Fortunately they are relatively long lived and so one bad year is not a total disaster. The whitefronts at Holkham, six or seven hundred of them, would probably fly on to Slimbridge in earlier years. Now they stay here because of the good food and the fresh water on the marshes. It saves them two or three hundred miles.

The pinkfeet are beautiful birds and I enjoy photographing them. With the rolling Norfolk countryside and the stubble fields they make a lovely picture. They get a lot of food from stubble fields – spilt grain and second growth. The picture of the sunrise with the geese flying through it – pinkfeet – is magical. I took it at 7.30am and there were thousands of them. Because of these wonderful wildlife sights Norfolk is becoming increasingly popular with tourists in winter as well as summer.

The old gravel pits at Snettisham were dug out during the Second World War. They are now owned by the RSPB and they too give spectacular views of wildlife from the Wash. When the tide comes in over the mud, thousands of birds go to roost on the shingle next to the gravel pits. There can be a few thousand redshank and up to 20,000 oystercatchers. It is another amazing winter spectacle and it makes you realise just how special this whole area is to wildlife.

BELOW: *Redshank and oystercatchers at the RSPB's Snettisham reserve.*
OVERLEAF: *Sunrise with pink-footed geese flying through it.*

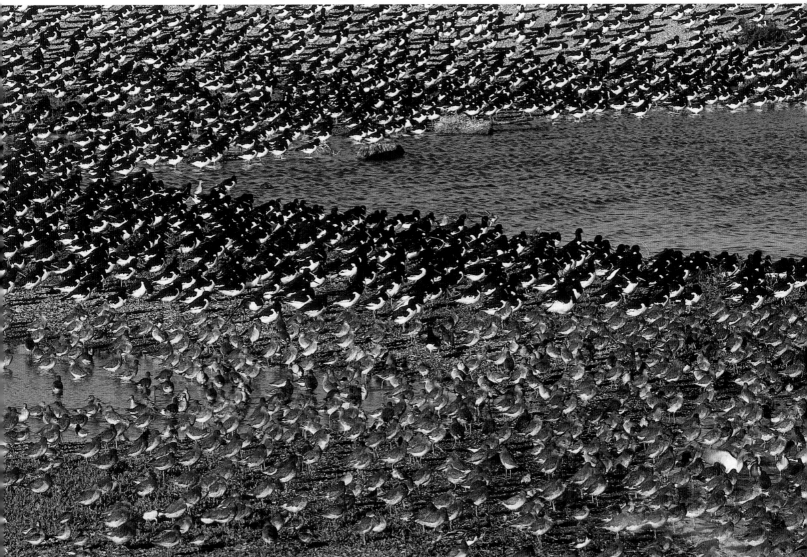

Knot – many still in breeding plumage.

Knot also join together in large, incredible flocks. The picture above of knot shows the early autumn migrants with quite a lot still in breeding plumage. Knot and grey plover on the Wash make the autumn and winter very special. They arrive from their breeding grounds in the Arctic, Greenland and Russia; they travel huge distances, some stay all winter while others move on to the west coast of Africa. At one time the Fenman didn't watch the flocks of knot, they tried to catch them – to eat them. As Thomas Bewick wrote: *'These birds are caught in Lincolnshire and the other fenny counties in great numbers, by nets into which it is decoyed by carved wooden figures, painted to represent itself, and placed within them. Much in the same way as the ruff. It is also fattened for sale, and esteemed by many equal to the ruff in the delicacy of its flavour. The season for taking it is from August to November, after which the frost compels it to disappear.'*

Later on, when the knot have lost their breeding colours and are in their ordinary winter plumage, they are grey on top and white underneath. They fly in large flocks and their aerial co-ordination is astonishing. As they turn in unison they show their topside and then their underside and so they appear to keep changing colour from grey to white. It is quite extraordinary. They are powerful and fast flyers, and seem to enjoy flying. As the tide comes in they all get up and fly around,

RIGHT AND BELOW: *Knot – first you don't see them, then you do.*

ABOVE: *Curlew in early autumn.*
LEFT: *A green sandpiper.*

even when they don't have to. It is as if they are simply enjoying themselves.

Flocks of curlew also come to the Wash; the picture above was taken in early autumn. They come down from the north and several thousand spend their winter in the area. We get a few common curlew nesting on the farm, as a breeding bird, which is nice; the breeders arrive back in early March. Overwintering visitors could nest in Norway or northern Scotland. They have a lovely bubbling call, so evocative of wild places – it creates a mental image of muddy estuary, salt marshes, and in summer – moorland and mountain. I would never eat a curlew – but for years they were regarded as a delicacy by 'fowlers' along the coast; in Suffolk it was even called the 'land pheasant'. Way back in 1275 the going rate was 3d (old pence) for a curlew and at the Coronation Feast of Henry VI the menu boasted, in addition to curlew, 'plover, larks, swan, heron, crane, bittern'. I've never been a fan of burgers but probably it's a good thing they are so popular these days.

The green sandpiper is a pretty little bird which now sometimes spends the winter with us in dykes, weirs and muck heaps – anywhere where there is a little flush of water. They look at first glance rather like a large swallow, with a white rump clearly visible when they fly away from you. They have a distinctive liquid call. They breed in Norway and Sweden, and in the Arctic circle. Sometimes they will breed in old nests of other birds – like blackbirds. At one time they would just pass through during spring and autumn; but some have been staying for the winter for the last 20 or 30 years. Whether this change has been caused by global warming – or simply a change of behaviour – who knows?

I photographed this ruff on migration too. There used to be a few which bred in Norfolk until the 1960s but now they are all moving through to Sweden and Norway, where there is a lot of water and wetland.

The bar-tailed godwit is another winter migrant. This one has lost its summer plumage.

A ruff in winter plumage.

83

ABOVE: *A bar-tailed godwit in winter.*
RIGHT: *The reflection makes it look as if this greenshank is crossing its legs.*

They breed far to the north and their display flights are really beautiful, with the male and female chasing round and calling all over the tundra. They often pass through here still in their breeding plumage. Sadly, they don't breed here although their close cousin, the black-tailed godwit, still does.

Due to the reflection this greenshank looks as if it is crossing its legs. They are graceful birds and I have seen them in the winter in Africa – and in summer in Scotland where some breed. They are powerful flyers, and have to be – to cope with the distances they cover. The old egg collectors – when it was legal – always regarded finding a nest as blue-ribbon day. They are apparently very hard to find as the bird slips off its nest well in advance of approaching intruders. We get them

stopping off at a little pond on the farm as they pass through in the autumn and we are always pleased to see them. The call is a number of fluting, liquid notes and I have often called them myself by whistling when they have been flying around. If there is water nearby they will come down and land, bobbing up and down trying to focus where the call is coming from.

We get lots of dunlin on the Wash too in winter. They form very large flocks – but not so massive as the knot. Many come from the north where they breed in the hills – there are still good breeding numbers in the Pennines. The bird in the picture is in its attractive breeding plumage, and I have to admit that I photographed it on its breeding ground in Siberia – we don't often get them on the Wash with its distinctive black belly. On their breeding grounds they have a lovely little twittering flight – calling and flying on fast wings.

BELOW: *A dunlin in its breeding plumage.*
RIGHT: *A herring gull trying to break a shellfish.*

When oystercatchers are looking for mussels, they need to be fast. I was watching them at Burnham when I took the picture on page 70. They have very powerful bills to open shellfish. The turnstone is much smaller and not so strong. Instead it is fast and quite brash. Here, the turnstones are poised and ready to dash in and try to steal or intimidate. The second the oystercatcher opens the mussel it has got to eat it, because if there is any delay a turnstone will pinch it; they are bold, bolshy little birds. They can't open the shells themselves and rely on the oystercatchers to do it for them. The gulls will drop their mussels to smash the shells, and they have to be quick to beat the turnstones too. You can see all this in several places along the coast – it is entertaining to watch. We usually regard both gulls and oystercatchers as being bold and uninhibited – it makes a change to see them under pressure from the little turnstone – obviously theft can be more rewarding than turning stones. The Norfolk name for turnstone is 'sea dotterel' due to its partial resemblance to the dotterel – which still passes through a number of sites in Norfolk while on migration.

The coast is always a good place to see special birds, and the waxwing is a very special bird. From late October, if there is a cold snap or a shortage of food on the Continent, there will be a sudden landfall of waxwings, and we will often get them first. They come from the Continent or Scandinavia and they land anywhere from Aberdeen to Kent. Some years there are parties of between 50 and 100. For several years it seemed that they had stopped coming, and there was a whole generation of birdwatchers that had never seen a waxwing. But all of a sudden they have started to come again. They nest in the northern forests of Russia and Scandinavia and are superb little birds. With this picture I was just lucky. I was sitting in the vehicle photographing in very low light. To improve things, I got out and set the camera up outside – the bird stayed in the bush and here's the picture. You have to be lucky sometimes. The waxwing is so attractive with its yellow tail and red wax-like wings that it looks too good to be true – I was very lucky and privileged to get this picture.

By contrast, the marsh harrier is another bird of East Anglia's coastal strip. When I first started taking photographs there were probably two pairs in the whole of East Anglia – now there are as many as 50. They are a large bird of prey and will nest in cornfields or reedbeds. They have between three and five chicks and are quite nervous birds. Hen harriers are far bolder; some of them spend the whole year here.

Marsh harriers hunt inland too. They take things as big as coots, young mallard and pheasants down to meadow pipits – a whole wide range of prey. They will clear out whole nests of young at a time – it's nice to have them but we don't want too many. The picture overleaf was taken as the bird hovered along a dyke near Holkham, where there were a few reeds; I drove further along and set the camera up and sure enough it continued hunting and I was able to take the picture.

LEFT: A 'lucky' picture of a waxwing.

By way of contrast the bearded tit is one of our smaller coastal birds. 'Coastal' in this case means the marshes behind the sea wall, or dunes, at places such as Titchwell, Cley and Minsmere. Bearded tits are among our most beautiful birds and as they fly they call with a strong 'ping, ping, ping'; which adds to their attraction.

The coast has always been famous for terns – with Blakeney Point always being an important centre. There are common terns, and also little terns, sandwich terns and a few pairs of Arctic terns. Summer is a magical time to go and see them. Over 50,000 people a year go out to Blakeney Point, showing how birds are vital to the economy of north Norfolk in winter and summer. The common terns nest in very loose colonies in the sand dunes, and they are not so violent as Arctic terns. If you walk through a colony of Arctic terns they attack you and can draw blood by pecking you on the back of the head. The birds in the picture are catching whitebait in the harbour at Blakeney. They love whitebait and so do I – whitebait are an important part of the Norfolk food chain for terns and pub menus alike.

LEFT: *A marsh harrier hovering along a dyke near Holkham.*
RIGHT: *A bearded tit – one of our most beautiful birds.*

Common terns nesting at Blakeney Point.

Black terns usually come through in early May, on migration. We don't always see them, but I have known a time when from Cley to Salthouse there were between 200 and 300 black terns flying about the dykes. Unfortunately, it is a bird that is becoming much rarer. It bred at Welney in the late 1960s for a couple of years; but numbers are down; they are little birds and nest in colonies that can easily be predated. The last colony I saw was in northern Germany. Three

magpies came into willow bushes beside it; there were about 20 pairs of terns and they really dive-bombed and chased the intruders. But the nests are out in the open and very vulnerable to magpies and crows. I would like to see black terns back, but I think it unlikely. They are fantastic little birds and it must have been marvellous when they nested in the Fens and East Anglia in the nineteenth century. We must do our best to make sure that we keep what we have left.

ABOVE: *Common terns catching whitebait at Blakeney.*
RIGHT: *A black tern.*

CHAPTER FOUR

Wetland and Stream

Wetland is exactly what it says – wet land – and it is superb for birds. With water being present it means food, vegetation, shelter, and places to nest. Wetland is also a photographer's or a conservationist's paradise. In my case it is a farmer's paradise and we have some excellent pieces of wetland on the farm. Even a small pond will attract a few moorhens and a pair of pied wagtails.

I am very lucky. Just as I live near north Norfolk, which is a paradise for coastal birds, so I am also close to Welney, which is the bird mecca of the Fens. The Welney Washes were created in the seventeenth century by a Dutchman, Cornelius Vermuyden, to drain the Fens. There are two large dykes or drains, that look like canals, with high banks – half a mile apart. The whole thing cuts 19 miles

ABOVE: *Cattle grazing in the Welney Washes.*
OPPOSITE: *A great crested grebe giving its chick a feather from its breast.*

across the Fens – taking all their surplus water and much of the storm water from Cambridgeshire and Bedfordshire. As a result it is a chunk of real wetland with high water levels and lush grass in summer, and floods in winter. It is a place of great beauty in all seasons, with a remote quality that is surprising as it is surrounded by villages and farm land. There are still herds of grazing cattle looked after by 'wash-shepherds'. In the winter there are thousands of swans and it is a major centre for seeing wildfowl and wetland birds. In the old days people would be wash-shepherds in the

summer and wildfowlers in the winter – shooting and trapping ducks, and even plovers, and sending some of them to London. During cold weather it was – and still is – famous for Fen skating.

The picture left is typical of winter and with swans going out from Welney Wash the swan numbers have built up well – over 1000 whoopers and well over 3000–4000 Bewick swans – a tremendous percentage of the world population. They all concentrate at Welney and so the reserves have been a great success and give the swans somewhere secure for the winter. Both the RSPB and the Wildfowl and Wetland Trust have reserves there, giving wonderful views of the wintering swans.

At the other end of the popularity scale, there are many moorhens and coots. When I was a boy at school I used to go down to the river and pick up moorhens' eggs, and then sit in class with

LEFT: *Swans flying out from Welney Wash.*
BELOW: *A moorhen – cleaned out by mink in many places.*

A coot and chicks.

soaking wet feet. We used to eat them, frying them on a little fire of twigs. I have to admit – they were very good. Moorhens are very territorial and they have a nice family habit. When the first clutch hatches and become teenage chicks, they don't tear off; they help mum and dad to feed the second brood. In fact the adults more or less leave them to raise the second brood, while they go off and nest again – for a third time. There are not the number of moorhens of earlier years, as they have suffered badly as a result of predation by mink – some of which were released in the first place by misguided 'animal rights' activists. Mink have cleaned out the moorhens and the water rails in our local river.

Coots are still common and their little chicks are like clowns when they first hatch with their red heads. Coots are very pugnacious birds, and will defend their young. They will even attack swans if they come too near during the nesting season. Later on in the year when they are diving and pulling the weed up from the bottom, gadwall will join them and feed with them. Gadwall are dabbling ducks – not diving – and so they make use of the coots' diving ability. I have seen this happen at Rutland Water and Cley. A pair will follow each coot round and as the bird dives, they will wait for it to bob up with the weed and tuck in; black headed gulls will also pick up the left-over scraps. The diving picture is of a tame coot in a water tank, but it shows the birds' diving ability very well.

The kingfisher is a real bird of wetland. It has been having quite a good time lately with a run of mild winters. The one pictured overleaf was on a little river close to home.

Little streams are very good for kingfishers. They are good for reed warblers too. Reed warblers will nest wherever there is a good stand of phragmites reed, the picture (on page 101) was taken in the Fens at a dyke full of

RIGHT: *A gadwall feeding with a coot and a gull.*
BELOW: *A coot diving in a water tank.*

LEFT: *A kingfisher with a fish for its young.*
ABOVE: *A reed warbler and family.*

these attractive reeds. There were 40 reed warblers' nests along this part of the dyke; nine with cuckoos in them and so they are very important for the cuckoo.

One of the famous birds of the Welney Washes is the attractive black-tailed godwit. Only a very few now breed there, which is a great shame as there were once at least 30 pairs. But the predation by carrion crows and foxes has been disastrous as have a number of late floods – swamping the nesting birds. The floods have been caused by the way the authorities drain agricultural lowland: also because large housing schemes have been built on flood plains. The resulting drainage causes flash floods at Welney which is devastating to all the ground-nesting birds. The floods push the godwits out to the ordinary farmland where there is even more predation. So we have a choice –

A black-tailed godwit.

carrion crows, magpies and foxes – or black-tailed godwits? There will always be foxes and crows – but will there always be godwits? I photographed godwits at Welney in the late 1950s before there was a reserve; their decline is a tragedy.

As well as the coast having redshank, there are also a lot at Welney, and many breed successfully. They are very jittery little birds and the moment you put your head over the sea-wall or bank, they send alarm calls out everywhere. The old wildfowlers didn't like them very much because they made such a racket around them and called them 'the watchdog of the marshes'. They are very beautiful little birds, and when they are about to mate the male has a tremendous wing display; he walks right around the female with his wings quivering and this can go on for several minutes. At one time we had them nesting on a little water meadow in the Brecks, but the carrion crows finished them off. Now we just have

A redshank – 'the watchdog of the marshes'.

one or two pairs: we do employ a gamekeeper, and the crows that he gets rid of on the farm benefit the pheasants and partridges as well as the remaining redshank.

Although ruffs are quite boring in the winter, in spring the males are transformed. They have occasionally bred on the Washes, and at Cley, but not very often. It is fantastic to see the ruffs in their extravagant plumage. There is a great variation in their colours, including ginger, white, black and grey. They dance and display to each other and then the female walks up. The males are flat on the ground, quivering with intent and she just walks by them. Nine times out of 10 she will go to the male with a white cape, very politically incorrect. In the Netherlands, where I took the photograph (overleaf), I've seen 150 ruffs all dancing, jostling and fighting; it was a memorable sight.

Not many people realise that the common snipe also has a fantastic display. Unfortunately the common snipe is becoming increasingly uncommon, with its population tumbling by 90%. The picture on page 105 was taken towards the end of the breeding season, and there are some young snipe there; they are just showing off and displaying to each other. Snipe have tremendous displays.

LEFT: *A male ruff in its breeding plumage.*
ABOVE: *Common snipe, which are becoming increasingly uncommon.*

I have seen them when they cock their tails up, put their heads down and go 'chip, chip, chip, chip', walking and chasing through the long vegetation. Ten yards further back nothing would be seen, but in a hide it is all happening in front of you. There are lots of these displays, and they are in addition to their display flight. That is where the air is rushing through two tail feathers, making a bleating note like a sheep – the country name for a snipe in Scotland is 'heather bleater'. They are very territorial, and know exactly where they have reached, even when doing their aerial display. The decline in the number of snipe has been caused because lots of land and little corners have been drained; in addition they are very vulnerable to birds of prey, particularly sparrowhawks. I have even found a little owl that killed snipe in the winter time. Snipe are quite fast flyers and so the birds of prey have to be alert to catch them. They are very attractive birds with long bills. When a bird of prey comes over the snipe will put its bill flat to the ground, with its rear in the air, and put a display of feathers up to make itself look twice as big. There is only one problem; it doesn't seem to work very well.

Not all is gloom and doom, and the story of the avocet is a great success story in the wader world. It returned to Britain just after the Second World War, to Suffolk, and has now spread out into the north Norfolk coast and into the Wash. Even Welney now has avocet nests inland. They are very aggressive and pugnacious for their size and grace and will drive off other wading birds. As a result they are not great favourites with the twitchers. They tolerate each other quite well, but not other birds; they will even see off ducks much larger than themselves.

The great crested grebe is another success story. They can be seen now in wetland over the whole of the country. I see them at Welney, in summertime they breed on the Great Ouse and the gravel pits have them. During the winter they even fish in the sea off the north Norfolk coast. I won the British Birds, 'Wildlife Photographer of the Year Award' with the picture on page 94 in 1985. It is actually feeding the chick a feather just plucked from its breast; some say they do this because chicks are fed small fish and the feather helps deal with the bones. They lay up to four eggs and the chicks are very comical with red faces. The eggs are white, but by the time they hatch they are stained a very dark grey-green because of the way the birds hop in and out of the water. The main predator of chicks is pike, and mink can also be a problem. They are not as aggressive as coots in defence of a nest; if they are disturbed they will cover their eggs and glide away. If they

The avocet – a success story.

106

don't cover their eggs then they become prime targets for the feathered egg thieves – magpies and crows. I took the picture with a 300mm lens, using kodachrome film.

I spent about five days at the grebe nest over a period of three weeks. Because of the hours spent it is important to be comfortable and wear warm clothes. If there are things happening I can easily sit for up to 12 hours in a hide. I take food, coffee and sandwiches with me and I sit on an angling stool. You have got to be comfortable, warm and dry, and the hide needs to be waterproof so that if there is a thunder storm you can sit it out and get some good pictures.

Welney is a perfect place for wildfowl. I like all ducks – rare or common – and I still get a thrill seeing ordinary widgeon, teal and tufted duck. Teal are very striking little ducks, especially in sunlight. There can be several thousand at Welney and I have seen flocks of 500. They fly like dunlin – moving and turning as one – it is marvellous. They remain in a tight pack, twisting and turning one way and then the other. When you see 200 teal turning over a small pond, showing the streaks of green of their wings and heads, it happens so quickly that it is impossible to photograph – yet it is a moment of magic that stays in your memory for ever.

The tufted duck is an attractive duck; there are not so many at Welney now, but they are doing well on all the gravel pits and reservoirs that have been created over recent years.

Teal – a marvellous sight when flying in a tight pack.

We had 11 pairs on the farm last year, on our irrigation reservoir and our ponds. It is a duck that has increased by 20% in the last twenty-five years. It is a cracking little duck. It is very similar to the American ring-necked duck, they are difficult to tell apart although the ring-neck has a little ring marking on its bill. When the tufted are pairing up there is a lot of fighting and displaying. It is good to watch these common little ducks – you

LEFT: *A pair of tufted ducks.*
BELOW: *Widgeon and mallards.*

ABOVE: *Whitefronts at Welney.*
OVERLEAF: *Bewick swans displaying.*

don't have to have rare ducks; the tufted are as attractive as any duck that might turn up and they are lovely to see.

Widgeon and mallards are very common ducks too, but they are very colourful and full of character. At Welney you can see between 20,000–30,000 widgeon flying and feeding. They have a superb whistling call that I always associate with wild, beautiful places. The widgeon in the picture opposite is male; they can congregate in large flocks in winter; they graze on grass – they are most effective lawn mowers – while mallard and teal are dabbling ducks. Their calls and displays, especially when they are pairing up, are fascinating to watch and Welney is one of the best places in the country to see them.

There are geese at Welney too. A 'whiffle' is when the geese fly in after seeing other geese feeding on a field from a thousand feet up. They want to lose height and so they start whiffling – they side slip from side to side – and sometimes even go upside down. A whole flock will whiffle in and lose 500 feet in probably a second or two and just fall out of the air; it is a spectacular sight.

All sorts of geese pass through Welney – whitefronts, pinkfeet, bean geese and grey lags. There are geese and ducks present throughout the year, but the winter is when numbers really build up.

A whooper swan family.

But Welney is most famous for its winter swans. The smaller is the Bewick – named after Thomas Bewick. When they first arrived the Bewicks used to be mainly in front of the hide, but then gradually as the larger whoopers increased in number the Bewicks stayed further back. Between 700 and 800 whoopers can be seen near the main hide of the Wildfowl and Wetland Trust – it is a memorable and spectacular sight on a cold winter's day. There are now up to 1600 whoopers at Welney during the winter having migrated from Iceland and Scandinavia. The Bewicks number 4700 and they come from Siberia, it is a long flight for a smaller swan – but the Bewick is the faster flyer.

Although Welney is a very special place for me there are many other places in Britain that can give wonderful wildfowl experiences in winter. I am just very lucky that Welney is almost on my doorstep. I am lucky too, to have known it before it was a reserve. It was Peter Scott who had the idea of creating the Wildfowl and Wetland Trust Reserve. It is a wonderful memorial to him that it has developed into such a great success story.

RIGHT: *Bewick swans coming in to land at Welney.*

CHAPTER FIVE

Highland and Moorland

I really enjoy visiting areas of moorland and high-land as it makes such a contrast to East Anglia. We are so privileged to have areas such as the Pennines, the mountains of North Wales and the Scottish Highlands as part of a country as small as Britain. The Cairngorms, when they have snow on them are really beautiful. It means that one day I can be experiencing the wildfowl spectaculars of the Fens; the next day I can be in almost Arctic conditions in the Highlands. I love Scotland and go there almost every year. The people are different too – forget what people say about the Scots, I always find them very warm, friendly, hospitable and generous – yes, generous – with their time and their 'wee drams'. From the road or the air the views are wonderful and I am always sur-prised that more tourists do not go to Scotland in the winter. I walk a lot too – going up to the high tops with their short turf, mosses and lichens – it is absolutely fantastic and I can walk up there for hours. The birds are different too; crested tits, ptarmigan and snow buntings, and then in summer ospreys and

OPPOSITE: *The River Tanar.*
ABOVE RIGHT: *The Border country from the air.*
RIGHT: *The 'high-tops' of the Cairngorms.*

dotterel. Scotland really is a naturalist's paradise – I don't think the urban Scots who run their Parliament know how lucky they are.

The old Caldonian pine forests are unique, with several almost Arctic species of birds. I love it where old trees have died and regeneration is taking place. You get a wonderful mosaic of heather, old trees, young trees, dead wood, new wood, beautiful old silver birches and areas of blaeberry which the grouse love so much. Although I am sad to say it, the pine forests of the Breckland are no comparison – they are regimented into plantations and look artificial. The areas of old Scottish pine forest are living entities in their own right; they are beautiful and the whole appearance and mood stays in your mind and ensures that you will always return to Scotland for more.

The many lochs of Scotland are haunting and rich in wildlife. You can get sea lochs and fresh water lochs with birds such as grebes and greenshank nesting.

OPPOSITE: *Loch Morlich in winter.*
BELOW: *Ancient Caledonian pine forest, one of Scotland's endangered habitats.*

Moorland and loch – ideal for wildlife.

The other main feature is simple moorland; but that too is so attractive with its own wildlife. Grouse – the red grouse and the whisky brand, must be two of Scotland's most famous symbols and two of Scotland's most important money earners. They bring a tremendous number of people into the Highlands to shoot. A lot of work goes into preserving and managing grouse and there are good years and bad. The heather is burnt in patches to produce new growth, as well as old, and that explains the mosaic pattern of many Scottish moors. It shows that it is a working, active grouse moor. Such a moor gives much-needed employment to rural Scotland and provides work for gamekeepers and general estate workers. Grouse flying low over the land, hugging the contours, make a wonderful sight. They make a thrilling sight if you are shooting around the 'Glorious Twelfth' 12 August – the first day of the grouse-shooting season. The birds attract shooting men from all over the world and they are very good to eat. I have shot grouse, but I did not enjoy it – I was thinking of their beauty all the time – and now I prefer to shoot them with my camera. The red grouse in the spring are fascinating to watch with the males displaying and calling 'goback, goback, goback'. Scotland has good numbers of grey partridge too – you can't call them English partridge there – particularly in

ABOVE: *Red grouse flying low over Scottish moorland.*

RIGHT: *The famous red grouse.*

Aberdeenshire and Fife. But even so, I think the red grouse has the edge when it comes to flying and shooting. The grouse is an amazingly hardy bird, and its nest will be covered with snow, yet it will carry on incubating and the chicks will hatch.

The osprey is the other famous Scottish bird – once shot to near extinction, but now back and doing well with up to 90 pairs

An osprey fishing – the one that didn't get away.

nesting in Scotland. The RSPB must take much of the credit for the return of this stunning bird. It returned to Loch Garten in the Cairngorms and the RSPB set up hides and telescopes and millions of visitors have now seen the birds. It was a wonderful example of education, conservation and public relations. Ospreys regularly visit the fish farm at Aviemore. My picture of the fishing osprey was actually taken in Finland. It took me a whole week to get this picture. I was in the hide every day

ABOVE: *An osprey with a fish.*
RIGHT: *Goosanders on their wintering ground.*

and took over 3000 shots to get this one fantastic photograph. It emphasises the point, I hope, that in bird photography you have to be persistent, patient and lucky.

Goosanders are less spectacular fishermen – but they are very attractive birds. They are the larger of the 'sawbills' – that means that their bill has serrated edges to help them hold the fish they catch securely. They are very good fishermen, indeed some salmon fishermen would say that they are too good – taking a lot of young salmon. They are very striking

ABOVE: *Goldeneye displaying in the sea near Berwick-upon-Tweed.*
RIGHT: *I just happened to be in the right place at the right time for this dipper picture.*

ducks, the males have attractive green heads; they can swim very fast under water. As a result they catch fish easily – perhaps more easily than the anglers.

Sea lochs and estuaries have their birds too. These goldeneye were displaying in the sea near Berwick-upon-Tweed. They nest in holes in trees and gate posts and all sorts of places, and the duck-lings jump out shortly after they hatch, yet they don't seem to hurt themselves even when they land on rocks.

By contrast the dipper can be found on anything from tiny moorland stream to large fast flowing river. It is fantastic just to sit and watch them: they wade into the water as if it were noth-ing and disappear – walking underwater, or they stand on a rock and throw themselves into the fastest flowing current. It seems as if they must be swept away, but they will pop up 30 to 40 feet upstream having walked against the current. It is amazing how powerful they are with their big long feet that can grip the bottom and allow them to walk. They eat anything aquatic – small fish, insects and larvae. They build their nests under bridges, rocks or banks, and they are still quite com-mon. They have suffered a 10% population decline in the last twenty-five years, but numbers appear quite stable at the moment. In the winter I have seen them on rivers, standing on the side of the ice where it isn't frozen before throwing themselves into the churning water – I always marvel at that – the water temperature must be very low. Their insulation is wonderful – better than that in my house. They don't need big rivers but they do seem to favour a fast flow. I just happened to be in the right place at the right time for this dipper picture and the pair had a nest just upstream. Thomas Bewick called the dipper 'the water ouzel' and wrote; '*The feathers like those of the duck tribe, are*

imperious to water whereby it is enabled to continue a long time in that fluid without sustaining injury. But the most singular trait in its character, is that of it possessing the power of walking, in quest of its prey, on the pebbly bottom of a river, and with the same ease, as on dry land.' I wish we had dippers in Norfolk but all our rivers flow too slowly.

A hundred years ago the common sandpiper was far more common than it is today and even nested in parts of lowland Britain. Now it has retreated to the Highlands and nests wherever there is a stream, along ledges and banks, on shingle islands that are covered with heather; around the edges of lochs and I've found nests on the ground and made of grasses and fine roots, I've found nests in a heather clump, in amongst the shingle, and in all sorts of places. They are fine little birds, always bobbing up and down the whole time. They have an attractive call too. They don't stay here, they migrate to Africa in the winter and it is always good to see them there.

The Slavonian grebe is one of Scotland's very special birds; it is the stronghold for them in the British Isles. When you go further north, to Europe and Scandinavia, they become very common. It is an absolutely superb little bird and just like the great crested grebe it makes a floating nest in the reeds. It is much smaller than the great crested grebe, but just as striking. It has red-currant eyes, golden ear hair tufts and it has an attractive display; all in all it is a cracking little bird. There is no record of it breeding in Britain until the last century and sadly, with global warming it could retreat further north again in search of cooler weather.

Another rare, but attractive breeder is the red-necked phalarope, breeding mainly in Shetland and the Hebrides. It is very trusting and tame and you can watch it from the roadside, almost within touching distance. The male and female arrive at the breeding

LEFT: *The common sandpiper.*
RIGHT: *The Slavonian grebe, one of Scotland's most stunning breeding birds.*

site together, with the female being more brightly coloured; she mates and lays her three eggs; the male is then left to brood the eggs and raise the family, while she goes off to have another love affair and does the same thing with another male until she has a few broods. Then the females team up together and migrate back to the Indian Ocean, the Persian Gulf and West Africa while the males are still tending the chicks – it is all rather an extreme form of feminism.

By complete contrast the capercaille is a large bird, almost as big as a turkey. It is one of the highlights of wildlife in Britain – one of its country names is 'The old man of the wood'; it is the largest grouse in the world. It has already become extinct in Scotland once and was success-

ABOVE: *The 'feminist' red-necked phalarope.*
LEFT: *A capercaille doing a 'flutter jump'.*
RIGHT: *'The old man of the wood' displaying.*

fully reintroduced. Sadly, numbers are tumbling again and there are only about 1000 birds left. When the cock bird is displaying, during the very early morning (3.30am) it fans its tail out and it is spectacular. The hens fly into the display ground probably just as it is getting light. The capercaillie in the picture left is doing a 'flutter jump' which is a noisy jump, throwing itself into the air. It has white underneath its wings, so that if a hen is sitting 50 to 100 yards away she can see it. The fall in numbers has resulted from several factors. Predation by foxes and pine martens is significant. Bad weather can be a disaster, with the chicks suffering in wet cold springs. If they manage to rear two or three young

they are doing well: five is fantastic. Deer fencing has also been damaging – much of it put up by conservation bodies to protect regenerating forest, but as they fly through the woods at 4 to 5 feet high, they meet a 6-foot high deer fence and – splat – that is the end of one capercaille. It is tragic. Deer fences are now being taken down to help save the capercaille. I hope it is not too late. Sometimes during the breeding season there will be a rogue cock who will attack the postman, the paper boy or whoever invades his territory. They can give you quite a powerful bash with their wings.

The blackcock is another beautiful bird of the grouse family. The cocks are very vain and display to each other at 'leks' – you can have as many as 20 cocks at a large lek in April. When a hen bird appears there is a great crescendo of activity. The jumping and jousting gets more fever pitched with each male hoping to attract the female by his extravagant performance. The bubbling calls also

LEFT: *A blackcock in breeding plumage.*
BELOW: *Blackcock at the lek.*

ABOVE: *Ptarmigan at Glenshee.*
LEFT: *A hen ptarmigan sitting on nine eggs.*
The late snow has made her stand out like a sore
thumb.

intensify. It is a superb bird; in Scotland it is struggling but it is doing much better in the Pennines.

The ptarmigan is the hardiest of all grouse, rarely coming below the 3000 feet mark, and then only in the winter storms. They soon go back to the hill tops, where they live in the harshest conditions to which they are ideally suited. The picture left is of a hen ptarmigan sitting on nine eggs. In winter the plumage turns snow white – but she is in her summer plumage. The late snow has made her stand out like a sore thumb.

The picture opposite was taken at Glenshee. An eagle was flying along the crest of the hill, putting all the ptarmigan to flight across the valley. They were all in their wintertime white and it was a very memorable sight.

In Norfolk, every spring, we still get the brief annual arrival of the 'dot plover'. That, too, is a bird of the Scottish hill tops – the attractive and elusive dotterel. It must be something about the Scottish air, because this is another case of the female laying the eggs and then leaving the male to incubate and rear the young. The sitting bird here is the male. They are very tame little birds and were once targeted by egg collectors. They are

RIGHT: *A male dotterel incubating eggs.*
BELOW: *The 'dot plover' in breeding plumage.*

now targeted by bird photographers, but you must get a licence to photograph them at the nest as they are a totally protected species. The first time I photographed dotterel I had an old reflex camera and took pictures of the sitting bird just a few feet away from the nest. Now, with large lenses, I stay well away from them. We still get the occasional 'dot plover' moving through the farm and I love to see them.

Golden plover go as high as the dotterel, and there are many of them, all over the Pennines and through the Highlands of Scotland. Moorland is their breeding habitat and they are still quite successful, making them one of the most common waders in the world. Because of its call we call it 'the whistling plover'. The ones in Scandinavia have a lot more black than the British birds. The further north they go the blacker they become. They are among our most beautiful birds and we get large winter flocks of them in Norfolk and Suffolk. It is another bird, along with golden eagles and merlins, that requires a licence for photographing on or near the nest.

I photographed the eagles at their nest on the Mull of Kintyre, just after the male had brought in a stoat – sometimes eagles will take fox cubs too – so some predators do not have it all their own way. The female is easy to distinguish from the male as her bill is half as big again. Golden eagles are doing very well in Scotland now and are a magnificent sight.

LEFT: *A female golden plover in summer plumage.*
RIGHT: *Eagles at their nest on the Mull of Kintyre. The male has just dropped a stoat into the nest.*

OPPOSITE: *A merlin with a young meadow pipit for its hungry young.*
ABOVE: *The crested tit, one of my favourite birds.*

The merlins make a complete contrast by way of size. We get them on the farm occasionally in winter. They are very fast flyers – being slightly smaller and stockier than a kestrel. This one, in the Highlands, was feeding its young on small meadow pipits – between 20 and 30 a day. It always flew to this rock to have a look around before moving on to feed its four hungry young.

I have saved one of my favourite birds to almost the last. In Britain, the crested tit is only found around Speyside, although on the continent it is widespread. I love this picture and when I look at it I am immediately back in those wonderful old pine woods.

But although this book is of birds, Scotland has a lot of good animals too. The red deer stag is a fine animal – but in Scotland there are too many of them. In Norfolk we have red deer too: they are not found in Scotland's numbers, but they are much bigger as the quality and quantity of food is so much better.

The red squirrel is another of Scotland's special species. They are wonderful animals. It is so good to see them taking food that has been put out for them. Twenty-five years ago we had red squirrels in Norfolk. It is important that the squirrels of Scotland are not over-run by grey squirrels as they have been in most of England.

Finally, another bird I associate with Scotland – the puffin. It is not a bird of highland or moorland but I like the picture and so I have included it.

OPPOSITE: *A red deer stag.*
RIGHT: *Red squirrels are still holding their own in Scotland.*
BELOW: *Puffins – not highland or moorland but attractive.*

Afterthought

Although there is much gloom and doom around at the moment, things may not be as bleak as we tend to think. Yes, things are bad and much more should be done for conservation, but it is surprising how some species seem to thrive, even in adversity. The obvious example is the collared dove. Whereas the populations of many species have plummeted, the population of the collared dove has increased by 782% and it has become an attractive feature of our countryside.

With global warming there are several other species which could easily move into Britain and colonise. Some are lovers of water and wetland, and so with rising sea levels there will be plenty of choice of places to settle – perhaps even central London.

The next attractive newcomer could be the European bee-eater. It is a very beautiful bird and can be seen at the moment in Spain and southern France. It would be a welcome addition. The only trouble is, of course, that global warming may not give us the warming that most people think. If warming does occur, then some experts believe that we may then lose the warming effect of the Gulf Stream. If the Gulf Stream does move away from Britain's west coast, then instead of warming, we may cool, and our climate might become like that of Quebec and Newfoundland, as we are at the same latitude. We enjoy a much better climate because of the warm sea currents coming up from the south.

The common crane is another bird that not only could arrive, but should already be here. It is a very slender, graceful bird and there are a few in East Anglia. However, their numbers seem static and it does seem that the natural process should be given a helping hand. This could be achieved with a sensible release programme – allowing a number of controlled releases where the habitat is right. Few people would object to having such a striking bird arrive in their area. Strangely, nearly all the releases and introductions at the moment are predators such as the red kite in England and

OPPOSITE: *European bee-eaters – British birds with global warming?*

139

OPPOSITE: *The common crane – still uncommon in Britain.*
ABOVE: *Spoonbills could be breeding here soon.*

Scotland, the sea eagle in Scotland and the osprey at Rutland Water. It is almost certain too that there have been illegal releases of goshawks. So why not a legal release of the common crane which poses few threats to our indigenous wildlife?

Spoonbills are already regular visitors. They are very attractive, distinctive birds, and from the shape of their bills they can never be mistaken for any other species. During mild springs, spoonbills can be seen at Titchwell or Cley along the north Norfolk coast and they can quite often be seen at Minsmere in Suffolk. It is a superb bird that we never used to see and it can only be a matter of time before it starts to breed here. It will be a very welcome addition to Britain's breeding birds.

Already little egrets have arrived and are breeding. They have spread here from southern Europe and Africa and are doing very well; it must be hoped that the spoonbill will follow suit. It seems inevitable too that the black-winged stilt will start breeding in Britain before too long. There has been a long-staying bird at Titchwell for some time, and a few years ago a pair actually bred at

Holme – rearing two chicks. In many parts of Africa avocets and stilts seem to get on well together. Avocets are now doing very well here – so why not the black-winged stilt as well?

The crested lark is not as spectacular as the black-winged stilt – but it is an attractive little bird in its own right. It likes drier and warmer conditions than the skylark – it is a real bird of arid country. If global warming really does warm Britain – or at least southern Britain – then it is highly likely that the crested lark would do very well here.

Another attractive newcomer could be the penduline tit. It is a very pretty little bird, looking like a cross between a bearded tit and a long-

tailed tit. It builds a nest hanging in the branches – hence its name – and it would be very welcome. They are the most likely birds to be among the first colonisers of a warming Britain and then there are black woodpeckers, honey buzzards, Cetti's warblers and marsh warblers – in fact marsh warblers are already breeding here.

So, the future seen through the eyes of some birds is not as bleak as it could be. Yes – we will certainly lose some much-loved species – but others will come and add richness and beauty to our countryside.

ABOVE: *A crested lark.*
LEFT: *A black-winged stilt.*
OPPOSITE: *A penduline tit at nest.*

Chris Knights is Vice-Chairman of the Countryside Restoration Trust and is a great supporter of the Game Conservancy, the RSPB and the Norfolk Wildlife Trust. His form of farming fits in naturally with the philosophy of the CRT which believes that farming and wildlife should co-exist – to create a living, working countryside. If you have enjoyed this book and would like more details of the Countryside Restoration Trust, please write to The CRT, Barton, Cambridgeshire CB3 7AG. E-mail info@crtbarton.org.uk, or visit the website www.crtbarton.org.uk

The late Gordon Beningfield – countryside artist and campaigner – was the CRT's first Vice-Chairman. He was also a patron of Butterfly Conservation.

Bird's Farm Books has published a book of bird and wildlife paintings by Gordon Beningfield as a tribute to his life and work. Signed copies of *Beningfield's Vanishing Songbirds* can be obtained from Bird's Farm Books, Barton, Cambs CB3 7AG. For every copy sold a donation will be made to the Gordon Beningfield Memorial Appeal to buy a farm in Dorset – run by the CRT as a tribute to the life and work of Gordon Beningfield.

Beningfield's English Orchard will be the last book published of Gordon Beningfield's unpublished work. It will be a companion volume to *Beningfield's Vanishing Songbirds* and will be published in 2003.